Copyright © 2024-2025 by Pippa Bird

All rights reserved. No part of this book may be reproduced or transmitted in any form or by any means, electronic or mechanical, including photocopying, recording, or by any information storage and retrieval system, without permission in writing from the publisher.

ISBN: 9781763833869

First Edition

In the heart of the bush where the gum trees sway,
lived Terrance the Tarantula, who loved to play.

But try as he might, and crawl as he may,
Terrance was always late to the fray.

His friends would gather, laughter filling the air, but poor Terrance just couldn't get there.

Through grass and leaves, he took so much time, arriving quite late, and missing the climb.

One day, Cookie the Kookaburra, kind and bright,
saw Terrance struggling with all his might.

With a flap of his wings and a twinkle in his eye, he said, "Terrance, my friend, let's give this a try."

"Come, Terrance, I offer you a lift.
For inclusion is the greatest gift.
Hop on my back, and we'll fly over the trees,
You'll be on time, with the greatest ease."

Terrance hesitated, then climbed on his wing.

And off they soared, like it was the start of spring.

Cookie flew high, and Cookie flew low,
with Terrance aboard, enjoying the show.

They arrived at the gathering, right on the dot.

Terrance was thrilled, this was quite the spot.

"Thank you, dear Cookie, for your thoughtful lift.
Now I can join in, it's the greatest gift!"

His friends cheered loudly, happy and bright,
For Terrance was with them, from morning to night.

Now every day, beneath the sun rays beam,
Terrance and Cookie are quite the team.

With a lift from his friends, he never runs late.

For Terrance the Timely,
life is just great.

With laughter and love, they all play and sing,
such friendship like this, is a magical thing.

Pippa Bird
Calm Kangaroo

www.ingramcontent.com/pod-product-compliance
Lightning Source LLC
LaVergne TN
LVHW072118070426
835510LV00003B/122